Diane

May you enjoy this
Art of my Leadership Experiences
as I continue my journey
on the Mission field

Adera Loster
12/7/18

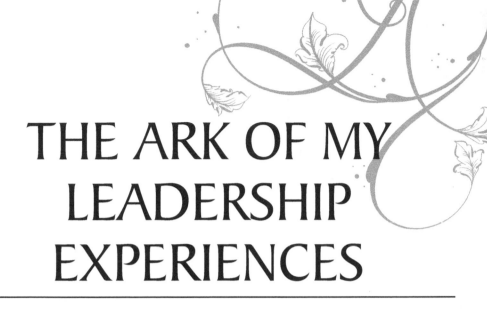

THE ARK OF MY LEADERSHIP EXPERIENCES

21 PEARLS FOR LEADERSHIP

ADENA WILLIAMS LOSTON, PH.D.

ISBN 978-1-64114-953-2 (paperback)
ISBN 978-1-64349-519-4 (hardcover)
ISBN 978-1-64114-954-9 (digital)

Christian Faith Publishing, Inc.
832 Park Avenue
Meadville, PA 16335
www.christianfaithpublishing.com

Printed in the United States of America

This book is dedicated to my son,
Gilbert Williams Loston III

CONTENTS

DISCERNMENT

REVELATION

TAKE ONLY WHAT
GOD GIVES YOU

You must learn to accept only what is God given. It is without question that when it comes from above, He will provide the increase. We frequently want positions, things, and even people in our lives that are purely our wants with no relationship for God's purpose for our lives. Consider the position that you most desire. One Sunday afternoon on my usual journey, I was driving across the Chesapeake Bay Bridge, and it was swaying as it normally does, it was a point of clarity. The thought rushed through my mind, this is not why you came here. I knew then this assignment with NASA was over. I wanted to return to the educational arena and redirect my public service, I began to apply for various positions. But my strategy was quite different from other applications for positions earlier in my career. I prayed to my Father to close the door that I was not supposed to walk through. Knowing that being in a leadership role would not be easy, I certainly did not want to enter into such a position without the Lord on my side. So when the position at St. Philip's College was offered to me, I was confident that this was my special assignment.

I recall going to this Christian placement agency early on in my career seeking to secure a higher level position so I thought. The gentleman coach, that sat with me and reviewed my resume, said to me that my next position would not come through him; but would come from a contact, a phone call. So when I received a phone call one afternoon saying that the general counsel from NASA was coming to Houston, and would like to visit with me, I didn't grasp the significance immediately. I rather stated, I don't think so. After the fourth phone call, I relented and agreed to meet with the general counsel on his visit to Houston. We met in the visitor's center conference room at the Johnson Space Center on the very last day of our summer schedule. During the summer months, the college would operate on a 4 ½ day work schedule so since I was done at noon on Fridays, I agreed to meet the general counsel at 1:30 p.m. on that Friday afternoon.

In leaving the position of president at San Jacinto College South to accept the position at NASA and leaving NASA to accept the position of president at St. Philip's College, I relied upon my Father to lead, guide, and direct my path. My steps were ordered. No leader can/ should go it along. Moses leading the children of God from pharaoh's bondage relied upon God's anointing. You should take only what God gives you!

> *For I know the plans I have for you, "declares the Lord," plans to prosper you and not to harm you, plans to give you hope and a future.* Jer. 29:11

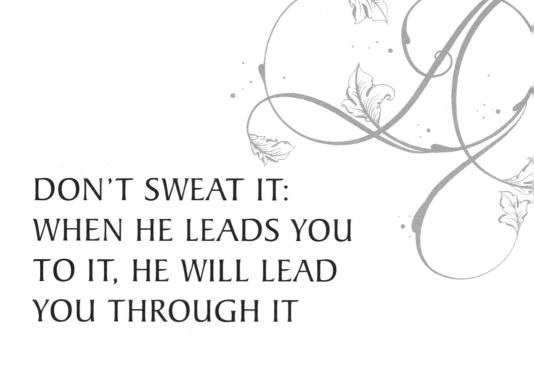

DON'T SWEAT IT: WHEN HE LEADS YOU TO IT, HE WILL LEAD YOU THROUGH IT

Sometimes, it's through a spoken word of confirmation, a song, a card, or the Holy Spirit you will be sustained throughout your trials. I remember my first administrative appointment. The supervisor had desperately wanted to hire another individual; but the president selected me for the position as supervisor over non-credit programs. So while it was a brief celebration in this appointment, my supervisor continued to show her displeasure with my appointment. In sharing my good news with my mother, she congratulated me and warned me that the same voice that extols you will also tear you down in the same day.

My supervisor provided me with a typing stand (approximately 24 inches X 36 inches) as my desk and placed it in her office to keep an eye on me. So as not to be out done. I purchased a live plant to sit on my tiny desk and brought in a family photo to also place on my desk. This only left enough space about the size of a sheet of paper to work with. I dressed the part of a supervisor always in business suits. I showed up daily on time mostly early and left late always after 5:00 p.m. If someone wanted to reach me via phone, they would telephone her office and she would pass me the receiver. I demonstrated no sign of frustration. I was determined to endure. I think bringing in the plant and photo for my tiny desk messaged that I was getting comfortable and in it for the long haul. After a period of time, she suddenly found an office for me upstairs away from her. This whole set up proved to be more distracting and frustrating for her than for me. She was now sharing her private office, her telephone, and entertaining company which proved quite awkward for her. I ultimately reported to this individual for ten (10) years although sometimes it felt like forty years. My resolve remained steadfast and my Sunday morning alter prayers were solely dedicated to this supervisor until one morning God changed my heart. Need I say more about that?

My father cared for me during this period just as he did for the children of Israel when they were in a foreign territory.

> *So do not throw away your confidence; it will be richly rewarded. You need to persevere so that when you have done the will of God, you will receive what He has promised.* Heb 10:35-36

THE SEAT OF POWER

In a new CEO position, I recall walking into my conference room for one of my meetings with the new team and clearly the seat at the head of the table was already taken, occupied. I wasn't certain if this was a deliberate act; but I decided to show no visible reaction. The gentleman sitting at the head of the table, inquired, "Oh, am I in your seat?" He motioned to get up and I placed my hand on his shoulder to push him back down into the chair. I calmly replied, "No, wherever I sit is the seat of power!" As you might imagine, there was a complete hush over the room and as you also might imagine, that gentleman never sat at the head of my conference table ever again and for that matter, no one else ever attempted that stunt. That evil spirit was no more.

When Jesus went into the synagogue and began to teach, the people were amazed at his teaching because he taught them as one who had authority, not as the teachers of the law. Then a man in their synagogue who was possessed by an evil spirit cried out, "What do you want with us, Jesus of Nazareth? Have you come to destroy us? I know who you are—the Holy One of God!"

Jesus answered, "Be Quiet, Come out of him!" The evil spirit shook the man violently and came out of him with a shriek. The people were all so amazed that they asked each other, "What is this? A new teaching—and with authority!" He even gives orders to evil spirits and they obey him? News about Him spread quickly over the whole region of Galilee.

> . . . *But you were washed, you were sanctified, you were justified in the name of the Lord Jesus Christ and by the Spirit of our God.* 1 Cor. 6:11

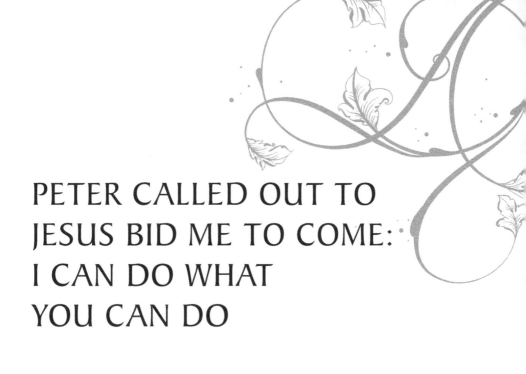

PETER CALLED OUT TO JESUS BID ME TO COME: I CAN DO WHAT YOU CAN DO

C an I do what I see others doing? Peter saw Jesus walking on water and called out to him. Observing the actions of others does not mean that you too will have the capacity to do the same. It can have disastrous effects.

It was with much joy and adulation that I accepted the campus leadership position in a community college. This was delivering me from a tumultuous time in California during the Rodney King riots. So I was quite happy to have this position. In relocating to El Paso, I had plans to initially travel to El Paso, secure living quarters, and then return to Los Angles to retrieve my household goods over the Labor Day holidays.

During this short time span, my boss and the governing board had a serious disagreement and they appointed his administrative assistant to the position of president. This is the person that I had observed in my short tenure as the note taker for the president during our leadership meetings. Over the three-day weekend, all had changed, the assistant was my new boss. Having served as the aide to the president and now assuming that they could do the job proved to be quite problematic for all concerned. Not only did the individual lack credibility, they lacked experience, lacked judgmental skills, lacked leadership capabilities which resulted in a disastrous impact on the organization, administration, faculty, staff, and students. The individual was ultimately removed.

The individual even lacked in comprehension skills in knowing that when you are told that your services are no longer needed, you don't protest and tell the governing body that I'm not leaving. Ultimately, this leader was locked out of their office. Thinking that you can do what others do, may look easy but appearances may be just the tip of the iceberg.

Peter thinking that he could do as Jesus had done by walking on the water attempted to do the same. Though they carried the same physical structure, the similarities could not be more different. Peter, a man of faith; Jesus is the truth, the way, and the light.

I've learned to wait for God's elevation.

> But those who hope in the Lord will renew their strength. They will soar on wings like eagles; they will run and not grow weary, they will walk and not be faint. Isaiah 40:31

A CHANGE IN LEADERSHIP

Each time I have changed leadership positions, I always go back and read the book of Joshua. I am reminded when Joshua took over the leadership reins after Moses. No small tasks!

In my interview, he asked so what do you think about this. I said "I liken this to an analogy that I thought about on the plane ride from Houston to DC." I gave this accounting: "I have my 100 X 100 sand box with my castle, my moat, my drawbridge, and protectors all around me and you want me to come and play in your 1,000 X 1,000 sand box, I have no castle, no moat, no drawbridge," and he joined in by saying your protectors will become your detractors. I expressed that I had no network in his industry.

Leaving San Jacinto College South to go to NASA Headquarters in Washington DC was not an easy decision. It was leaving over thirty plus years in education to go to a totally new industry. As I had expressed to the administrator, I am neither a scientist nor engineer and NASA is a science and engineering agency, and I am too far down the road to create a credibility problem for myself. His response was, "I have thousands of scientists and engineers, and we need someone that knows education." I said, "I know education, I have over thirty years of experience," and his response was, "I know that's why we are calling you."

Moses had to leave the comfort of the Pharaoh's Palace to lead God's people!

> *I was young and now I am old, yet I have never seen*
> *the righteous forsaken or their children begging bread.*
> Psalm 37:25

THREE DAYS

How soon they forget!

After celebrating one of the most successful years—the same yellow stick-on "low morale" was placed on the parking lot board again during a planning session. The parking lot was a space created for matters to be addressed that were not on the agenda. We raised $1,000,000 for student scholarships, celebrated our oldest living one hundred two-year-old alumna at homecoming, hosted a Women's Tea for our new endowed scholarship donors, and our founding president being named a saint, a Holy Woman through our Celebrating a Saint. The Low Morale stick-on had been placed on the parking lot for the last several years we think by the same person. It was always just those two words. This year would be no different. However, we did address the ownership piece for folks figuring out what makes you happy and then figuring out how to do just that. We also had varying managers to speak about the various activities and celebrations that take place monthly in their respective areas to recognize employees.

The morale responsibility was no longer an issue for the CEO but also the responsibility for the "victim."

Within three days of God parting the Red Sea and the children of Israel seeing ten plagues rained down on the Egyptians, they forgot that God had spared them and safely delivered them out of the hands of their oppressors, their enemies, their former slave masters.

They forgot that God had sent the deliverer to speak to the pharaoh on their behalf.

They forgot that God turned the Nile River into blood causing the fish to die and the river to stink such that none could drink water from the river and yet the Israelites had been warned to store up water.

They forgot about the frogs, gnats, flies, dead animals, sores, hailstones, locusts, and darkness and most assuredly, they forgot about the deaths of all their firstborn Egyptians.

You have heard it said you are only as good as your last success (oh shucks). Moses, the prophet who communicated directly with God, provided leadership for the multitude out of slavery, one of the greatest leaders, ultimately failed to reach the Promised Land. Moses struck the rock to bring forth water. God had instructed him to speak to the rock to bring forth water. His failure to follow this set of instructions proved to be a catastrophe. The punishment meted out resulted in him not going over into the Promised Land, the land flowing with milk and honey. People will forget about ten/forty years of successes and remember the last blunder or create a mental image that is unintended or not so.

The people forgot 400 years of bondage, their pleadings to be rescued, only to be delivered and within three days of crossing the Red Sea, were now requesting to return to pharaoh's rule, pharaoh's dictatorship, pharaoh's bondage, ungodly leadership.

How soon they forget. This phenomenal is Biblical!

> *The Lord will fight for you; you need only to be still.*
> Exodus 14:14

HE DIDN'T TELL SARAH

When Abraham took Isaac to be sacrificed, Abraham didn't tell Sarah, his wife. He took Isaac and two servants. Sarah would not have been overjoyed at the thought of sacrificing her only child, the child of promise for which she waited so long. Remember, she had even grown impatient by sending Hagar, the handmaiden, in to her husband and they conceived of Ismael. So there is no doubt that Sarah would have been conflicted had Abraham revealed what he was being led to do.

When the forty-fourth president of the United States pondered the hunt and considered the raid on Osama Bin Laden in Jalalabad, Afghanistan, he did not tell all of his leadership team. It was with limited knowledge that this mission was planned and carried out. I don't think that he did not trust his team or Abraham did not trust Sarah. I think that the risk of the team sharing with others was too great and Abraham simply trusted God more.

While all may have the same desire to achieve the end goal; all may not have the capacity, intentional focus, stamina, clarity of purpose, and acute precision. With deliberate intentions, as leaders, we must sometimes guard strategic decisions. All simply cannot carry out the mission with the same commitment, dedication and loyalty of purpose. It is like the sight of blood; everyone does not particularly care to see; everyone does not particularly care for the witnessing in the administering of medication.

The president called his predecessor, the forty-third president of the United States, after the successful mission was accomplished even though this had been a long standing mission of the forty-third president and his team.

My father didn't tell his mostly white cliental what his true price structure was when he said, "I have a special price just for." Growing up in Vicksburg, Mississippi, for a period of time, my father was the only black self-employed licensed master plumber. When individuals would call and seek his services, they would frequently call him a nigger. We were either nigger or colored (not yet black or African-American). Daddy would charge people according to the way they talked to his children. His decision was strategic. He attempted to restore some dignity with the child that had to take the message. He would tell his clients, "I have a special price just for you" with the child that took the message present. People never knew that the price elevated when we were called inappropriate names; and if the clients said please and thank you to his children, his price would decline and sometimes, daddy would say "no charge."

Some decisions are truly on a need to know basis. When being led by God, you should not be entering into a debate with another man or attempt to be vetting the process. God's plan does not need or require a Monday morning quarter back.

Guard strategic decision!

> *Many are the plans in a man's heart, but it is the Lord's purpose that prevails.* Proverbs 19:21

DIFFICULT
DECISIONS

Constantly, for five years, I was confronted with difficult decisions. When I accepted the presidency of San Jacinto College South, I became the second president. I was not prepared nor had I given sufficient thought to the consequences of being number two in the presidential lineup. First, I came to appreciate the fact that the first president had hired all of the employees and secondly, they all seem to struggle with divided loyalties. Being number two could have been manageable except for the fact that when the president stepped down, she took a seat on the governing board and frequented the campus almost daily or calling various employees and administrators (now members of my leadership team) to get an update and render an opinion of what should be happening. This continued for five years, my entire tenure in the position.

Once, an administrator came to my office to report that the former president and now board member was sitting in her chair at her desk. She wanted to know what she should do. The former president would frequently show up to my meetings on the campus. The unfortunate thing is that my predecessor would not sit quietly, but always had an opinion rather it was about strategic direction, budgetary matters or personnel matters. In the inauguration of our first fast pitch softball game and new field, I was scheduled to throw out the first pitch until my predecessor called and said she would be doing that. It was not until game day morning that the show down was averted. I had gone to the store and when I returned home, my son had taken a phone call. He said that person that has been bothering you will not be bothering you today, she is in the hospital. I thought, "Thank you, Lord." My coping mechanism became a regular routine. Accepting the concept as fact that we are all God's children, this person was my sister in Christ. So when I would see her coming, her hand or head popping up in my meetings, or receiving a late night phone call to brief me on her latest interferences, I would begin to pray. This is my sister in Christ, this is my sister in Christ. It was almost a chant to keep my mind clear. I am still amazed at my duration in this position. Later on down the road in my career, I was approached by a head hunter to determine if I was interested in a particular position. The head hunter shared this will be a great opportunity, you will be the second president at this fine institution. I could barely contain my thoughts, there was a rush of anxiety, a rapid fire of memory lane. Needless to say, I declined interest with all deliberate speed.

Moses's mother had a most difficult decision. When she learned of the pharaoh's edict to kill all male babies, she made a decision to send her son afloat in a wicker basket rather than resign to his certain death. Ironically and providential, Moses wound up in the care and kingdom of the one issuing the commandment for his death.

> *Yea thou I walk through the valley in the shadow of death, I will fear no evil. For thou art with me, thy rod and thy staff, comfort me. Thou prepares a table before me in the presence of mine enemies; thou anoints my head with oil. My cup runneth over. Surely goodness and mercy shall follow me all the days of my life and I will dwell in the House of the Lord forever.*
> Psalm 23:4–6

God will hide/protect you in the presence of your enemies. He will make your enemies your foot stool. Understand, the pharaoh's sister raised Moses with all of the riches and finest experiences that any child of a pharaoh could have imagined.

Like Moses being raised up in the very household that delivered the edict; I was being raised up and my leadership skills honed though for some would have been an impossible situation and certainly not for five years, half a decade. Prayer will give you the grace to be able to reframe the circumstances, not to focus on the uninvited guest; but rather to focus on we are all God's children and you are in the mist of your brothers and sisters in Christ. Reframe your difficult decisions. It's called God's Grace.

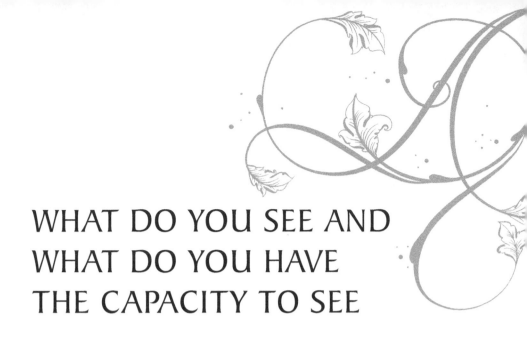

WHAT DO YOU SEE AND WHAT DO YOU HAVE THE CAPACITY TO SEE

David, the youngest son of Jesse, was overlooked by his father as a kingly possibility!

In selecting the next king of Israel, Samuel was dispatched to anoint one of Jesse's son. The Lord said to Samuel, "Look not on his countenance, or on the height of his statue; because I have refused him. For man looketh on the outward appearance, but the Lord looketh on the heart." Jesse made seven of his sons to pass before Samuel and Samuel said to Jesse the Lord has not chosen these. David was ruddy, with a fine appearance and handsome features. And the Lord said, "Arise anoint him for this is he."

When I considered the opportunity to work at the National Aeronautics and Space Administration, there was some trepidation. I invited my neighbor over to my home because he was truly a rocket scientist and worked at NASA. I had printed out pictures of all senior leaders, the associate administrators and the administrator of NASA. I placed a picture at each seat around my dining room table. So when my neighbor arrived, I asked his opinion. He asked what was going on. I said, "Look at these people at the table and do you see me sitting at the table with them and able to hold my own." He smiled, laughed and then said "yes, you can hold your own with them." It was my strategy for putting myself in the room with other senior leaders at NASA.

I had to have the capacity to see beyond my current presidency.

> *We live by faith, not by sight . . . Now it is God who has made us for this very purpose.*
>
> *And has given us the spirit as a deposit, guaranteeing what is to come.* 2 Cor 5:7, 57

THE MINORITY REPORT

I t all depends on what perspective you chose and whose you are.

Twelve spies were sent on a reconnaissance mission to assess Canaan, the Promised Land. The mission was to spy out the land ripe for takeover: see what the land is like, what the people are like—strong or weak; is the land good or bad; how is the soil—fertilized or poor. Bring back some of the fruit of the land. It took forty days. Instead, the spies were reporting back as to how they would be viewed by the opposition, the current inhabitants. Ten spies reported that if they attempted a takeover, they would be viewed as grasshoppers to the giants that currently occupied the Promised Land. Ten spies saw giants that could or certainly would annihilate them. They were definite obstacles. Two of the spies saw a land ripe with opportunities and ready for takeover. How is this possible to have such drastically different views/reports? They were optimistic in their assessment of the situation for it was territory already promised to them. Ten spies were overcome with their perceived inadequacies while two spies were overcome with potential! The ten presented a loss of focus, loss of direction, and a reversal of the mission. The capacity to vision is not always innate. However, as a leader, the capacity to vision and take bold steps is essential.

As a mid-level administrator, I noted the scheduling pattern for a very popular course being offered only two days a week—Tuesdays and Thursdays. So if the students were attending classes on Mondays, Wednesdays, and Fridays, they would never be able to take this very popular course. This pattern had existed for many years because this was the instructor's preferred schedule to only work two days out of the week. My minority report for offering on all five days challenged comfort zones, long established habits, and practices as well as treading in union territory. My boss asked me if I wish to continue with my fight to change the course offerings and take on the union, I took the minority position although my boss was weak in his support of my goal. We actually increased enrollment for this course and the faculty member after great opposition, opted to maintain control over this course by agreeing to teach five days out of the week. Additionally, by restructuring the offering patterns over the summer months, we saved over $130,000 in not having to secure rental space off site each summer. This course was the milk and honey for students not only attending on Tuesdays and Thursdays but also who attended Mondays, Wednesdays, and Fridays.

Perspective! What do you see and what do you have the capacity to see. With evidence all around, we sometimes focus on totally the wrong thing. We miss the significant.

It is a skill set that will garner you the label of often times having the minority report!

> *The Lord will make you the head, not the tail. If you pay attention to the commands of the Lord your God that I give you this day and carefully follow them, you will always be at the top, never at the bottom.* Deut 28:13

DON'T WORRY ABOUT BEING OVERLOOKED

God just saved you!

Jeremiah tells us that I know the plans that I have for you, plans to prosper you and not to harm you. Plans to bring you to an expected end.

When I was leaving NASA, I wanted to return to Houston. I had my home that I had left behind and it would be just so natural for me to return back to Houston. There was a position that seemed so ideal for me. It was a presidency at a local community college. Many years ago, I worked there. It is where I received my first administrative position as a supervisor. It was perfect in my mind. I had asked my pastor, to serve as a reference for me. After making it through the initial interview, the open forum and interview with the chancellor, my name was placed on the board agenda for consideration as president.

When I learned that the board took no action on the chancellor's recommendation, I was devastated, disappointed. I shared my disappointment with my pastor. He contacted one of the board members to gain insight. He then reported back to me that this was the same night that the Board of Trustees was buying out the chancellor's contract and the board had further instructed the chancellor to cease from making any major decisions. A major point that the chancellor seemed to ignore. While I had prayed and asked my father to close the door that I was not supposed to walk through, this surely could not have been correct. Patience, tolerance, endurance, and obedience must all be acceptable in any Godly endeavor.

Where He needed me most was at St. Philip's College.

Wait for the Lord and keep his way. He will exalt you to inherit the land. Psalm 37:34

HONORABLE
DISCHARGES

W hat does your core team look like? When I arrived at St. Philip's College, I counted approximately twenty-five individuals reporting directly to me as the president. This was incomprehensible. For the span of control was great, there was no way that each direct report could possibly receive immediate attention from me, their supervisor. A restructuring was definitely in order, and I reflected immediately upon the task of Moses when his father-in-law, Jethro, arrived on the scene and observed Moses attempting to tend to the immediate needs of the masses of humanity. It was impossible. He needed lieutenants. I needed a core team for certain less than twenty-five direct reports.

God has always been about demonstrating victory upon victory with less. He has never engaged the multitude to do His will. He only required twelve to spread His word. Consider the team. Honorable discharges are acceptable and should be preferred.

With any required task, the labor pool may be many or it may be few. When Gideon had an assignment, he had 32,000 volunteers show up. I am always mindful of God's battle plan; His strategic plan of action. Consider these 32,000; the feeding, clothing, and sheltering of the team members, not to mention the disseminating of information, operational and tactical plans as well as the assessment of adequate mental tools to carry out the mission. Everybody is not equally and similarly equipped.

With one single call for solidarity, are you with me, are you afraid/scared, 22,000 folks packed it in and went home. Why were they there in the first place? With this many going home, you must know that they were only there for show and nothing more perhaps just to see what was going on—too timid for the tasks. Scarcely, can you attend to operational and tactical plans when you are afraid. Your mental gymnastics will get in the way of you even hearing the plan and being attentive during the planning sessions.

The 10,000 that remained was still too large for our God to contemplate giving them the victory. For the 10,000 would possibly claim victory without acknowledging the help from above. So another elimination round was conceived. All were sent to the water for observation on their drinking skills. Selection of the team that will take you to victory is ever so critical. It is with deliberate intent that the team must be tested either through you or divine intervention. Every one cannot go to the next level. You may attempt to carry them, cajole them, or trick them into thinking this will happen by serendipity or chance; but both of you will be disappointed. By the time I had reached year five in my administration, the entire team save two had changed and the core team consisted of three vice presidents, six deans with two administrative support individuals for a grand total of twelve (12) team members including myself. Ultimately, Gideon's victory was won with only 300 folks. Honorable discharges will enhance efficiencies, save time and perhaps even save lives through less stress, high blood pressure or even heart disease. Offer or deploy honorable discharges!

> *Commit to the Lord whatever you do and your plans will succeed.* Proverbs 16:3

I'VE GOT YOUR BACK

How often have we heard it said, "I've got your back!"

When Jesus went to the Garden of Gethsemane, he asked Peter to watch with him. Peter most loyal and trusted fell asleep . . .

It can be lonely at the top. Humans will fail you. Your most trusted and loyal can simply fall asleep, although not literally, but their actions may be slow, a pregnant pause, nonresponsive or not at all. One of the most loyal and trusted direct reports proved to be the biggest disappointment. She was always there when needed, always trusted in carrying out an assignment. When I requested that she expand her duties temporarily, she disappeared from my office for two weeks. This is a person who began each day by checking in to say good morning and ended the work day stopping by my office.

In the reassignment of one administrator, I asked her to step in temporarily. She agreed and then added the caveat that she would think about it over the weekend then get back with me. Monday morning she did not visit my office (this was unusual and out of character). Monday at close of business, she avoided my office. There was the same avoidance on Tuesday. So I telephoned on Tuesday evening during the drive home. I stated that I had not heard from you. She agreed and said, "Yeah, I said I would get back with you after the weekend." I advised her that the weekend was over, and it was now Tuesday night. I then paid attention that she still did not come to my office that Wednesday morning. In fact, two weeks passed, and she was still a no show.

When she finally entered my office, on another pressing matter that she could no longer avoid, I invited her to sit down. I advised that although she had committed to an extended temporary assignment, that I could not ignore her behavior. While she seemed puzzled by my statement, I further explained to her that this was the first time she had set foot in my office in two weeks when her usual behavioral pattern was to visit every morning and every evening. So she was off the hook for consideration because although she had agreed, I could not ignore her actions. Rather than stand guard with me in leadership, this was the equivalent of my Peter falling asleep. I suddenly realized her weakness and her ability to commit was at best superficial or wanting to just not able to provide strength beyond her current comfort level.

Peter was willing, but the flesh was week. Jesus bared his burdens alone. We can do what we must do sometimes alone or look for support from a totally different direction. "I've got your back", is sometimes just a metaphor! God's got your back!

> *Peter replied, "Even if all fall away on account of you, I never will."*
>
> *Then Jesus went with his disciples to a place called Gethsemane, and he said to them,*
> *"Sit here while I go over there and pray." Then he returned to his disciples and found them sleeping. "Could you men not keep watch with me for one hour? . . . The spirit is willing, but the body is weak."*
> Matt 26:33, 36, 40-41.

SKIP THE CRASH COURSE, YOU NEED A TESTIMONY

The tendency to speed up your journey and move ahead more expeditiously to that higher ranking position is not always in the best interest of all concerned. It was not until Moses forsook his royal heritage and went down in the pits with his people to learn how they made bricks did he understand their peril and their plight. Esther prepared herself with twelve months of beauty treatments before she was deemed ready to meet King Xerxes.

When you skip a step, you have the potential to create a credibility problem for yourself. At some point in time when you have the ability to say: I have experienced this before, this is not new, I have had to address this before or let me tell you about how I handled this before, the outcome is golden. The same administrator that was the note taker for the president who became president, I witnessed even the facilities staff question her directives. There was a constant questioning of her guidance and direction. Not only do you create a credibility problem, your novice and inexperience guidance may cause unintended consequences for the organization. A part-time employee had misrepresented the facts in a particular situation, and I was given guidance from my new president to follow her directive; it seemed to never occur to the president that she should gather facts from both perspectives before taking action. Ultimately, her immediacy in responding to one person caused consequences for the entire organization and her new leadership agenda. She lost champions and supporters due to some simple basics—gathering facts.

Shortcuts are not always what God intends. Most often, we have a test in order to give a testimony. Testimony leads to credibility in any arena that you must perform in.

> *Do nothing out of selfish ambition or vain conceit,*
> *but in humility consider others better than yourselves.*
> Phil 2:3

THEIR CLOTHES DID NOT WEAR OUT

When you are a part of the master's masterplan, your resources will not be depleted. Because the children of Israel did not trust God, and failed to recognize the Promised Land in their forty-day journey, he added one year as punishment for every day that they explored the land. A forty-day reconnaissance mission became a forty-year odyssey. Although the children of Israel had to endure a forty-year-odyssey, not what God intended, their clothes did not wear out and their feet did not swell. They ultimately died off because of their refusal to believe and trust in God. However, for those that did endured the odyssey/journey because of their belief—Caleb and Joshua and the youth—they were cared for while others were dying off. God always provides for his children. You must take comfort whether you are in the desert with ravens being sent to feed you or Jesus sending his disciplines out to spread His word, God will provide.

How often have we heard it said that I am a Christian, this is sometimes proffered as wonderful characteristics to validate the hiring selection of a candidate. This one said she was a Christian. The only one to volunteer this piece of information—the minority report. So she must be great. Watch out, be on guard, you know the end result; if the individual must declare their Christian values as the lynch pin characteristics for hiring; then don't. If the characteristics are not evidenced through character references in their past behaviors, then their training is not complete. Their lessons in behavior and job performance are yet to be solidified. It is far better to have a trusted reference that details one's job performance and behaviors rather than the applicant's declarations about their Christianity.

For the few times early in my career that I was swayed by such declarations in an interview, I have quickly come to regret such hiring decisions. I would rather have the individual connect the dots by already having demonstrated Christian beliefs, ethical decision making, integrity, a value system, and moral compass rather than telling me and others how devote they may be in the interview.

> *And those he predestined, he also called; those he called, he also justified; those he justified, he also glorified.* Romans 8:30

STRATEGIC ALLIANCES/ UNHOLY ALLIANCES

We have often thought of strategic alliances by associating with the right person, group, organization, or agency. Affiliate organizations, associations, and even people can lead to grave disappointments. Solomon, the wisest man that ever lived, fell victim to his own strategic alliances. Solomon's strategy was to create allies through marrying over 700 women and acquiring over 300 concubines all with an intended purpose of securing his throne. His downfall came with acquiring not only the wives and concubines from potential enemies, he also acquired their cultures, practices, faiths, rituals, and their belief systems from many different alliances. He was overpowered by distant voices from the various providences; they brought along their idol gods, customs, and norms. He did not change them; they changed him. They proved to be unholy alliances. Solomon became compromised, sidetracked with unnecessary practices, distractions, customs, and practices from every wife for sure and possible even his concubines.

Be careful of your strategic alliances. There may be unintended consequences. This ill-conceived strategy caused him to lose his kingdom. He further lost his solid positioning with God.

Everybody is not on the same journey even though they may have the same stated purpose and goal.

Jim Jones led nearly 900 people in drinking Kool-Aid. Whether it was the well-known cyclist's affiliation with a certain doctor or his teammates affiliation with him, they are now all tainted. He was the champion of champions; the most recognized name in the Tour de France. Many wise and savvy businessmen, women, and friends of a friend sought out the well-known financial advisor that now sits in prison for over 100 years deemed to be the supposedly wisest investor. These proved to be truly unholy alliances.

Forming an unholy strategic alliance does not guarantee a strong ally or allegiance to accomplishing one's goal(s). It does guarantee that your message may be distorted, cause you to be distracted, and you may have to deal with unintended consequences while attempting to accomplish your goal. It is essential that you possess a value system, and maintain a moral compass, and a vector that guides you daily. In communicating with individuals, I am constantly praying Lord help me to see who is really there in front of me!

Seriously, consider your strategic alliances!

> *Blessed is the man who does not walk in the counsel of the wicked or stand in the way of sinners or sit in the seat of mockers. But his delight is in the law of the Lord, and on his law he meditates day and night . . . For the Lord watches over the way of the righteous, but the way of the wicked will perish. Psalm 1:1–3,6*

IT DEPENDS ON WHERE
YOU ARE COMING FROM
PERSPECTIVE IS EVERYTHING

When I arrived at NASA as the chief education officer, there was a divided faction. Some believed in the concept that students should nominate their teacher to be the next educator astronaut. Others felt that students lacked the knowledge, maturity, or sincerity to nominate their teacher. Some wanted NASA to engage a nation in inspiring a new generation of explorers thus increasing STEM majors. We had not had an educator in space since Christa McAuliffe. I recall in one meeting that one senior manager asked the question: What is wrong with students nominating their teachers? He viewed it as a shortcoming of those individuals who didn't agree with this perspective. Through my years of educational experience I was able to shed light. I was able to provide clarity why individuals were not too excited about the concept of students nominating their teachers to become an educator astronaut. This changed the color and perception of all engaged. I explained to the management team that students are not likely to always nominate their best teacher because the goal was to select the best teachers. I emphasized that students may nominate their favorite teacher. So the question came back to me about what's wrong with that. Then I explained that the favorite teacher, may be the teacher that does not require homework, may allow them to skip some assignments or gives extra points that are non-academic related.

They began to understand that a student nomination would not necessarily yield the best STEM instructor. I felt that my education and experience did provide greater insight for the rest of the non-educators in the room.

When Ruth followed Naomi back to her native land after the death of Naomi's husband and her sons, she had no idea that Naomi would provide her with guidance for another husband. She simply said entreat me not to turn back; where you go I will go, where you lodge I will lodge, your people will be my people, your God will be my God, where you die I will die, and where you are buried, I will be buried. May the Lord deal with me ever so severely if anything but death separates us. Naomi had a perspective on mating that Ruth did not. Naomi's advice to her daughter-in-law, Ruth, was to wash and perfume yourself and put on your best clothes; note where your kinsman-redeemer lays down and lay at his feet. He will tell you what to do. As a result of her listening to her mother-in-law, Boaz, her kinsman-redeemer, responded honorably to claim Ruth. They produced Obed thus beginning the genealogy of David.

Perspective is everything!

> *"So Boaz took Ruth and she became his wife. Then he went to her, and the Lord enabled her to conceive, and she gave birth to a son. The women said to Naomi: "Praise be to the Lord, who this day has not left you without a kinsman-redeemer. May he become famous throughout Israel!"* Ruth 4:13-14

A STICK TURNS
INTO A SNAKE

U se what is in your hands!

Moses was given a stick that became his staff. This staff became a snake which was to be used as evidence of miraculous signs that God sent him to speak to the pharaoh of Egypt. But before going into the pharaoh of Egypt, Moses first was instructed to assemble the elders of Israel and speak to them. God had promised to bring them up out of their misery, bondage of Egypt into a land flowing with milk and honey.

I believe that we all have God given talents, skills, and abilities and if we fail to use our God-given talents, you are committing a sin. I believe that if it passes through my hands—any assignment—it must be appreciably better. I have a responsibility to make the situation or circumstances better. This concept I used to push my son to apply himself in all his endeavors beginning with school work. He was taught to prepare his homework not for the teacher, but as though he was going to present it to God. "Do as if unto the Lord" would be my guidance. This simple belief provided momentum for the journey, allowed me to encourage myself and my son was an honor student.

Use what is in your hands!

> *Now about spiritual gifts, brothers, I do not want you to be ignorant . . . Now to each one the manifestation of the Spirit is given for the common good.* 1 Cor 12:1, 7

IT IS NO SECRET
WHAT GOD CAN DO

I can do all things through Christ who strengthens me.

One late afternoon, the secretary left without locking the front office door. So after 6:00 p.m., I was still working in my office and a gentleman entered and asked if he could speak with me. I explained that it was late after hours and I was headed home. I apologized that the door was left unlocked. He expressed that he truly wanted to get my opinion as president. I again insisted that it was too late, and I was headed home plus it was my dinner time. He offered to take me to dinner which I immediately declined. After much insistence about wanting to get my opinion about his decision point, I agreed to meet at a restaurant not far from the campus. He stated that he had a decision to make and began to explain his dilemma.

He was being offered an opportunity to pursue his master's degree at a certain university. Under the assistantship, he would be required to teach classes and they would in turn pay for his graduate degree. He wasn't sure that he should accept the assistantship because the funds were through a set aside program for minorities. I immediately spoke up and said it sounds like you have a wonderful opportunity in front of you. They are offering you the assistantship because you are black. You will not keep it because you are black, you will have to perform. I think it is a great opportunity and you should take it and demonstrate your skills and abilities.

As soon as I uttered those words, it was like a light bulb came on for me. I had an offer on the table from NASA, but had not responded to their opportunity to serve as the associate administrator for education at headquarters in Washington, D.C. So the next morning, I telephoned the NASA administrator. His administrative assistant connected me to his cell phone as he was on his way to the office but stuck in traffic. I told him that I was ready to commit 110% to joining his team. However, in joining his team, I understood that I was leaving a leadership position to join someone else's team. I expressed that in joining his team I knew that he would always have three choices: to accept what I would bring to him in totality; to reject in totality or to modify. He said I hope that we would be in agreement. I expressed that I just wanted him to know that I was aware he had the same choices as I did as a leader. I did make one special request; that he would not micromanage me. Just tell me what is expected of me and then allow me to go and do. He agreed that would not be a problem. We talked for the rest of his trip to the office.

I think the visitor to my office was just a conduit to get me to focus on the offer and opportunity that the Lord had placed before me. Lord, open my eyes so that I can see!

Trust in the Lord with all your heart and learn not on your own understanding. Prov 3:5

SUCCOTH:
A TEMPORARY
DUTY STATION

When Jethro, the priest of Midian, Moses' father-in-law and father to Zipporah, arrived in the wilderness, he heard about all the good things the Lord had done for Israel in rescuing them from the hand of the Egyptians. He said praise be to the Lord, who rescued you from the hand of the Egyptians and of pharaoh, and who rescued the people from the Egyptians. He then had to witness Moses attempting to address the needs and concerns of God's chosen people. Jethro set up a tent as his living quarters and established a temporary home—Succoth.

My time at the National Aeronautics and Space Administration was an opportunity of a life time. But I was still a single parent mother. The thought of me without a paycheck when this assignment was up was not palatable. I needed some insurance; hence, I needed a career Senior Executive Service position. This career status insured that when the administration changed, I would still be guaranteed a position; although not necessarily the same position as chief education officer. So when the tenth administrator of NASA left to pursue an opportunity in higher education, the new administrator was now free to bring in his own senior management team just as I had arrived to support the 10th Administrator of NASA.

In the transition, I was assigned to Goddard Space Center Wallops Flight Facility as the Director of Education and Special Assistant for Orbital and Suborbital Projects. When I arrived in my new office, the immediate thought came over me that this is Succoth, a temporary duty station. I took out a yellow stick-on and wrote the word Succoth on it, and placed it on my desk. It remained there throughout my tenure. My secretary never inquired. The only person to inquire was the cleaning lady. She wanted to know what did that mean. I said when I leave, I will tell you. The few boxes that I unpacked I left them empty in the corner. So when it was time to leave, I just retrieved the boxes from the corner and repacked the few things that I bought there. I did linger on my last night because I wanted to be certain to keep my promise to the cleaning lady. So I explained to her that I always felt that this was a temporary duty station. We spoke about God's plans and said goodbye.

When He issues a command, a new assignment, a relocation— He gives you the ability to do so.

And we know that in all things God works for the good of those who love Him, who have been called according to His purpose. Romans 8:28

PROVIDENTIAL HAND

We had a very special December graduation ceremony at the local coliseum. Our interim Mayor was the speaker, and we had two African-American males as soloist. One sang the national anthem and another sang "Just Ordinary People." Both gentlemen sang beautifully. Following our graduation ceremony, one of the singers, returned to the robing room and reception area where the graduation party met prior to the ceremony. I complemented him on how beautiful he sang the national anthem and then inquired about his academic status and plans following his graduation. He stated that he wanted to transfer to a university; but did not have the money to attend school. As I received his message, I was troubled by his comments. He continued to remain in my mind. As we were preparing for university recruiting visits to the college, I sent for him. We scheduled an appointment, and I tried to determine how we could assist this young man in fulfilling his college completion goal.

Prior to his appointment, I had the staff to develop a list of universities that had four-year degree programs in music which was his area of interest. I also contacted a university music department chair who referred me to another individual that would be able to address voice scholarships. I was advised that there were limited funds for scholarships in this area. By the time he and I met, I still did not have anything definitive to tell him much to my disappointment. However, we visited and he told me that he had a 100% scholarship through the military; but lost it due to his allergies and asthma.

I informed him that a state university had a recruiting trip scheduled for St. Philip's College on Friday, January 30, 2015, and I wanted him to come. He did attend the recruitment event. At the close of the event, I was invited up to pull names of students out of a hat as scholarship recipients. I refused as I laughingly said I didn't want the pressure of pulling out the names. One young lady from the middle of the room shouted out: "I know that's right." The president from the visiting university insisted that it had to be me to select the students. With much reluctance and trepidation, I moved to the front of the room. Before reaching into the bag to pull a name out, I said to my Father, "Lord, let this be a providential hand." As I reach in and pulled out a name, the first name that I selected and read out loud was the young man I had invited to come. In front of all individuals, I witnessed and later shared with all the goodness of God and His providential intervention in this whole scholarship selection process. As a further testimony, the band director was present and hearing my testimony made his way over to us, said that he also had music scholarships to give away. I only knew that the young man could sing, but then he expressed that he played four instruments. They were then off to our Fine Arts Building for him to demonstrate his skills. He now had a scholarship to the university beginning Fall 2015.

This was a true providential hand!

> *Do not be anxious about anything, but in everything, by prayer and petition, with thanksgiving, present your requests to God.* Phil 4:6

ABOUT THE AUTHOR

D r. Adena Williams Loston is a product of the segregated South raised in Vicksburg, Mississippi. She attended the summer Freedom Schools created in the early sixties. Raised by parents who promoted the necessity of acquiring a college degree and a vocational trade while also requiring Bible study, Sunday school, Vacation Bible School, BTU, junior choir, and regular church service attendance. As a result of attending Alcorn State University, an Historically Black College, she was not cast into a mixed environment until attending graduate school at Bowling Green State University in Ohio. Her professional career catapulted her to many first. For almost forty years, she was either the first African-American or the only African-American to serve in her capacity as she advanced in her career. During her tenure at NASA, as an associate administrator and chief education officer, she was the highest ranking African-American female in the agency. Throughout her life's tenure, her most important role has been the mother of one son, Gilbert Williams Loston III. He has been her most important product and her most important project.

CPSIA information can be obtained
at www.ICGtesting.com
Printed in the USA
LVHW09*0503200818
587420LV00004B/4/P